let's talk about

BODY

BOUNDARIES,

CONSENT &

RESPECT

A book to teach children about body ownership, respectful relationships, feelings and emotions, choices and recognizing bullying behaviors

by Jayneen Sanders
illustrated by Sarah Jennings

For Mr Coonan, who always gave this little girl time,
and made her feel valued and respected.

J.S.

Let's Talk About Body Boundaries, Consent and Respect
Educate2Empower Publishing an imprint of
UpLoad Publishing Pty Ltd
Victoria Australia
www.upload.com.au

First published in 2018

Written by Jayneen Sanders
Illustrations by Sarah Jennings

Jayneen Sanders asserts her right to be identified as the author of this work.
Sarah Jennings asserts her right to be identified as the illustrator of this work.

Designed by Stephanie Spartels, Studio Spartels

ISBN: 9781925089196 (hbk) 9781925089189 (pbk)

A catalogue record for this
book is available from the
National Library of Australia

Disclaimer: The information in this book is advice only written by the author based on her advocacy in this area, and her experience working with children as a classroom teacher and mother. The information is not meant to be a substitute for professional advice. If you are concerned about a child's behavior seek professional help.

Note to the
READER

Teaching young children about body boundaries,
both theirs and others, is crucial to a child's growing sense
of self, their confidence and how they should expect to be treated
by others. A child growing up knowing they have a right to their
own personal space, gives that child ownership and choices as
to what happens to them and to their body. It is equally important
a child understands, from a very young age, they need to respect
another person's body boundary and ask for their consent when
entering their personal space. This book explores these concepts
with children in a child-friendly and easily-understood manner,
providing familiar scenarios for children to engage with and discuss.
It is important that the reader and the child take the time required to
unpack each scenario and explore what they mean both to
the character in the book, who may not be respecting
someone's body boundary, and to the character who is being
disrespected. It is through these vital discussions that children
will learn the meaning of body boundaries, consent and respect.
Learning these key social skills through such stories as
Let's Talk About Body Boundaries, Consent and Respect and
role-modelling by significant adults can, importantly, carry
forward into a child's teenage years and adult life.

Your body belongs to **you**, and you are the boss of it.

You are very special. There is no one exactly like you!

Everyone in the world has a **body boundary.** Your body boundary is the invisible space around your body. This space may be invisible but that doesn't mean it isn't there. No one should come inside your body boundary without you saying it's okay.

Sometimes we call our body boundary our body bubble.

Try this! Stand tall and then with your finger outline your invisible body boundary.

Look at this boy. He is trying to
hug his little sister.

Does she look happy about it?
Do you think she wants to be
hugged? How can you tell?

Here is what the boy should have done ...

Can I have a
hug please?

Yes! You can!

The boy should have **asked** his little sister for a hug.
This way the little girl can answer — because, after all, it's **her** body!

The little girl has two choices. She can say "Yes", or she can say "No".
If she chooses to say "No", then the boy should *respect that choice
and **not** hug his little sister.

No, thanks.

If the little girl chooses to say "Yes", then a hug is absolutely fine. That's because **both** people agree. Both the little girl and the boy are happy about the hug.

*Do you know what RESPECT means? Respect means you understand another person's wishes, and you care about them and their wishes. Respect is a very important word.

Sometimes a person may not be sure when another person asks them for a kiss or a hug. They might say, "I'm not sure I want a kiss." Or they might not say anything at all!

When a person says, "I'm not sure", or they say nothing at all, this is **not** a "Yes". The person has not given their **consent**. Consent is another important word for you to know. Consent means you have said "Yes", and you have **happily** agreed to the hug or kiss.

Sometimes kids say "Yes" to kisses and hugs when they **really** don't want a kiss or a hug. This might be because an older child or a teenager or an adult has asked them. It is always important to say **exactly** what you want.

Remember, it's your body and what you say goes! You can say "No" to kisses and hugs if you want to. You **can** say "No" to an older child, teenager or adult.

If you don't want to kiss or hug someone, you can give that person a hi-five or shake their hand! It is YOUR choice to make.

15

And even if you say "Yes" to a cuddle or someone holding your hand, you can ask them to stop at any time. Just because you said "Yes" doesn't mean they can hold your hand as long as they want to. If, at any time, you don't want a person to hold your hand or cuddle you, then that person must respect your choice, and **stop** when you ask them to.

Sometimes you might want to hug your baby brother or sister. And even though a baby can't speak, you can tell if a baby wants to be hugged or not. If the baby likes your hug they will gurgle and smile, and sometimes they will lean into you.

If they don't want a hug, they might cry or have a sad face or try to push you away. You have to look out for these things because a baby cannot tell you with words. We all have to respect a baby's body boundary too!

Every person is different. Some people like hugs and kisses and holding hands, and some do not. Some people like a hug one day but not the next. Just because a friend at school said it was okay for you to hold their hand on a Monday, does not mean you can hold their hand the next day and the next day and the day after that! You still need to ask each time if it's okay. You still need to ask for their consent.

This boy's older cousin wants him to ride on his bike with him.
Do you think the boy wants to go on the bike? How do you know?

That's right! The boy's face tells us.

Does the boy have to do what his older cousin tells him to do?
What should the younger boy do?

That's right! He could say, "No. I'm not going with you."

What should the older boy do now?

Yes! He should say something like, "No problem! Maybe
next time you can come with me."

But what should the younger boy do if his older cousin does **not** listen to him — if he does **not** respect his wishes?

Yes! That's right! He should tell an adult on his *Safety Network!

You are not a "tattletale" if you tell an adult on your Safety Network when a person does not respect your body boundary or listen to your wishes. That person did not show you respect, so you have every right to tell someone you trust.

Sonny's Safety Network

Mother

Grandpa

Teacher (Mr Ross)

Neighbor (Jenni)

*A Safety Network is made up of three to five adults that you trust. These are adults you could tell anything to and they would believe you. One should not be a family member.

Most of the time we all **love** to have cuddles and kisses from our family, and the friends we know well. But remember you can always say "No" to cuddles and kisses, and to people coming inside your body boundary any time you like. Your body is **your** body and what you say goes!

Everyone has a body boundary – babies, toddlers, children, teenagers and adults all have body boundaries.

Respect is a very important word. We need to respect people's body boundaries and we need to respect people's choices too.

This boy is playing in the sandbox at school. He is playing with a green bucket and a spade. Look! What is the other boy doing?

That's right! He is trying to take the bucket away so he can use it.

Is he doing the right thing? What does the boy in the blue hat need to do?

That's right! The boy in the blue hat needs to ask if he can use the bucket. He might say, "Can I use your bucket please?"

The boy with the green bucket has three choices.
Do you know what they are?

1. He could say, "No. I'm sorry, but I'm using the bucket right now."

2. He could say, "Yes. You can take the bucket."

3. Or, he could say, "We can share the bucket."

Whatever the boy with the bucket chooses, the other boy needs to **respect** his choice.

Waiting for our turn is also very important. Look! This girl is waiting in line at the school canteen. Another girl is pushing her out of the way and trying to take her place in the line.

What should the girl in the line say?

She could say, "Stop! Don't push in front of me. You need to wait your turn."

The other girl needs to learn to wait. She needs to line up like the other children. Sometimes we just have to wait our turn. It might make us angry but we need to find a way to calm down. A good idea is to take some big deep breaths. This will slow your angry breathing down and help you to feel calm.

What could the girl in the line do if she is too scared to say anything? That's right! She could tell an adult on her Safety Network.

We all have feelings. Sometimes we feel happy or sad or worried or scared. And sometimes we feel angry. Look at this boy. He is angry because the girl is going on the slide first. He is so angry he has stepped inside the girl's body boundary and pushed her.

What should the boy have done instead?

Yes! He should have waited for his turn.

Sometimes children get angry or pushy or even go inside another person's body boundary when they don't want them to. If this happens to you what should you do?

That's right!

1. You can say, "Stop! You are inside my body boundary."

2. You can tell an adult on your Safety Network if the person doesn't listen to you.

If you are the person who is feeling angry, the best idea is to talk to an adult who will listen to you and who can help you to calm down. Getting angry and then hitting or pushing someone is never the answer. It is **not okay** and it is not showing respect.

Every day you are growing older and learning new things. You are learning how the world works, and how people play and have fun together. You are learning to be kind and caring, and how to respect each other and how to keep safe. There is so much to learn!

But always remember!

1. You can say "No" to people who come inside your body boundary when you don't want them to, and if they don't listen to you, then you can tell an adult on your Safety Network.

2. People need to respect your body boundary and you need to respect other people's body boundaries too.

3. Your body is your body and you are the boss of it!

And remember ... there is no one exactly like you!

Discussion Questions for Parents, Caregivers and Educators

The following Discussion Questions are intended as a guide, and can be used to initiate an open and empowering dialogue with your child around body ownership and boundaries, consent, respect, respectful relationships, feelings and emotions, choices, and recognizing bullying behaviors. These questions are optional and/or can be explored at different readings. However, they will assist you and your child to unpack this important topic, and to explore both the helpful and unhelpful behaviors presented in the book. As you read the text, and discuss both the questions and the illustrations, it is equally important to encourage your child to talk about their feelings and emotions, and to assist them in developing empathy and understanding towards others. Throughout these conversations, it is also important to value your child's input and listen to their voice. Encourage and praise your child's positive responses and reassure them that it is a person's behavior that is often unhelpful rather than the person.

Pages 4-5

Ask, 'What does it mean when we say, "Your body belongs to you"? Are you the boss of your body? Why do you say that? How are you the same as these children? How are you different?' Say, 'Tell me something that is special about you.' Ask, 'What is your favourite thing to do? What are three things you are good at? Is there anyone else in the world exactly like you? Why do you say that? A person may not look like you but can people feel the same way as you? What kind of feelings might you have that are the same as someone else's feelings?'

Pages 6-7

Say, 'Let's stand up tall and use our finger to draw around our body boundary.' Ask, 'Why do you think a person's body boundary is important?' Note: for a book specifically focusing on body autonomy see *No Means No!* available at www.e2epublishing.info

Pages 8-9

Have your child answer the questions at the top of page 8 and follow their lead based on their answers. Draw out from the discussion that the little boy has come inside the girl's body boundary without her permission. You could ask, 'Is the boy inside the little girl's body boundary? Should he be inside her body boundary without her permission/saying it is okay? Why do you say that?' Ask, 'Can the little girl say "No" to a hug? Why do you say that?'

Pages 10-11

Encourage a discussion around the word 'respect'. Children are not too young to use and understand this term. Point out when someone shows another person respect in daily life. This will further help your child to understand the term, for example, if Child A asks Child B if they can play a game with them and Child A says 'No', Child B has to respect their wishes.

Pages 12-13

Discuss the word 'consent' in relation to your child's body and in general. Children are not too young to use and understand this term. Point out when someone gives their consent, for example, you might ask if you can help your child tie their shoelaces, and when they say 'Yes' happily, point out that they have given you their consent.

Pages 14-15

Point out to your child that they can say 'No' to a child, older child, teenager or adult if they don't want them to come inside their body boundary. Young children need to understand that they do have that right.

Pages 16-17

We need children (and adults) to understand that consent can be withdrawn at any time. This is very important for your child to understand as they grow into a teenager and an adult. Practicing and understanding this as a young child will reinforce this concept. Point out to your child that all people are different, and some do want to hold hands or hug and some do not. Let your child know it is okay if a friend doesn't want to hold hands or hug. It is their choice and it is not a reflection of how they feel about you.

Pages 18–19

Ask, 'Have you ever hugged a baby? What did the baby do? If you had a younger brother or sister or cousin could you just walk over and give them a hug? Why not? What should you do instead? Babies can't talk, so how do we know if they really want a hug or a cuddle?'

Pages 20–21

Ask, 'How are people different? How are they the same? What does it mean when we say that we have to ask a person for their "consent"? If you ask to hold a person's hand and they say "No", what might you say in return? If they say "Yes", what can you do now?'

Pages 22–23

Ask, 'Do we always have to do what an older person says? Sometimes we can say "No" as we have choices. When might we say "No" to an older person or a child the same age or younger?'

Pages 24–25

Ask, 'What is a Safety Network? Who is on your Safety Network?' Say, 'Let's draw an outline of your hand and write the names and phone numbers of the people on your Safety Network.' Ask, 'What is a tattletale? Is it okay to tell someone on your Safety Network when you feel unsafe? Why do you

say that?' Note: for an excellent children's book on personal Body Safety including information on Safety Networks and Early Warning Signs see *My Body! What I Say Goes!* available at www.e2epublishing.info

Pages 26–27

Ask, 'Look at the picture on page 26, how are the people greeting each other? Do they look happy about the greeting? Why do you say that?' Say, 'Point to two people who are inside each other's body boundary.' Ask, 'Do they look happy about the hug? Why do you say that? Before they gave each other a hug, what do you think they might have said?' Say, 'Come on! Let's outline our body boundary again!'

Pages 28–29

Go through the questions with your child. Follow their lead in the discussion.

Pages 30–31

Have a general discussion about respect and what it means. Talk about choices we make and why the boy has three choices when he answers. Ask, 'What would you have done if someone asked to use your bucket?' Discuss that saying 'No' can be okay if the child is using the bucket and needs it for their project. Talk about how the answer will depend on the situation, but the key is that the child in the blue hat asked to use the bucket, and that he respects the other boy's choice.

Pages 32–33

Ask, 'Do you think the girl who is pushing in front of the other girl is doing the right thing? Why do you say that? Was the other girl right to

say, "Stop! Don't push in front of me. You need to wait your turn"? Why do you say that? What would you do if someone pushed in front of you? Have you ever had to wait your turn? Was it hard to do? Tell me what happened.'

Pages 34–35

Ask, 'How are you feeling today? Why do you think you are feeling that way? When do you feel happy/sad/angry/ excited/worried/scared, etc? Should the boy feel angry because the girl is on the slide first? Why do you say that? Why is it never okay to push someone?' With your child, practice standing in an empowered stance. Have them hold out their hand and say, 'Stop! You are inside my body boundary!' and/ or 'Stop! I don't like that!' Ask, 'If the person doesn't listen to you or you feel worried, what should you do? Have you ever been angry? What did you do to calm down?' Note: instruct an angry child to take some deep breaths in and out, and on the out breath, blow hard as if they are blowing onto a hot drink or some soup.

Pages 36–37

Ask, 'What have you learnt from this book?' Note: you could write down the key messages your child provides if they are a reader and reread these at any time. Alternatively, have your child draw some key messages or have a further chat about the messages contained in the book. To end the session, you could have your child draw a picture of themself and write underneath: 'I am the boss of my body! There is no one exactly like me!' With your child, discuss all the wonderful, empowering and amazing things about them, and how these things make them unique.

Books by the Same Author

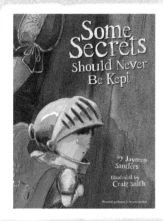

Some Secrets Should Never Be Kept

This book sensitively broaches the subject of safe and unsafe touch, and assists caregivers and educators to broach this subject with children in a non-threatening and age-appropriate way. Discussion Questions included. Ages 3 to 11 years.

My Body! What I Say Goes!

A children's picture book to empower and teach children about personal body safety, feelings, safe and unsafe touch, private parts, secrets and surprises, consent and respect. Discussion Questions included. Ages 3 to 9 years.

How Big Are Your Worries Little Bear?

This book was written to help children overcome fears and anxious thoughts by providing them with life-long skills in how to deal with anxiety. Discussion Questions and hints to help anxious children included. Ages 3 to 9 years.

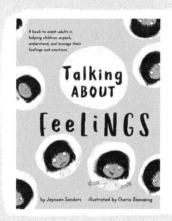

Talking About Feelings

A book to assist adults in helping children to unpack, understand, and manage their feelings and emotions in an engaging and interactive way. Discussion Questions included. Ages 4 to 10 years.

Resilience

This charming story about a little girl called Emmi uses verse and familiar childhood scenarios to encourage children to be resilient, persistent, and to help them bounce back from adversity. Discussion Questions and activities promoting resilience included. Ages 4 to 9 years.

You, Me and Empathy

This charming story uses verse, beautiful illustrations and a little person called Quinn to model the meaning of empathy, kindness and compassion. Discussion Questions and activities to promote empathy and kindness included. Ages 3 to 9 years.

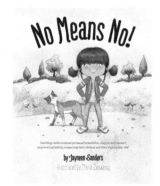

No Means No!

A story about an empowered little girl with a strong voice on all issues, especially those relating to her body! A book to teach children about personal body boundaries, respect and consent. Discussion Questions included. Ages 2 to 9 years.

Body Safety Education

An essential step-by-step guide for parents, caregivers and educators on how to protect children from sexual abuse.

For more information go to: www.e2epublishing.info

CPSIA information can be obtained
at www.ICGtesting.com
Printed in the USA
BVHW021605210621
610036BV00002B/10